COUNT THE MONSTERS!

WELCOME TO

COUNT THE MONSTERS

GOOD LUCK!

HOW MANY MONSTERS HAVE **TWO EYES?**

There are
8
monsters with two eyes!

HOW MANY MONSTERS HAVE **HORNS?**

There are 7 monsters with horns!

ARE THERE MORE RED MONSTERS OR PURPLE MONSTERS?

There are **7** purple monsters and **9** red monsters

So there are more **red monsters!**

HOW MANY MONSTERS HAVE **STRIPES?**

There are 6 monsters with stripes!

CAN YOU COUNT THE ORANGE MONSTERS?

There are 5 orange monsters!

HOW MANY **MONSTERS** ARE HERE?

There are 9 monsters here!

HOW MANY MONSTERS HAVE **TAILS?**

There are 4

monsters with tails!

ARE THERE MORE HAPPY MONSTERS OR UNHAPPY MONSTERS?

There are **7** unhappy monsters

There are **9** happy monsters

So there are more happy monsters!

HOW MANY **PINK** MONSTERS ARE HERE?

There are **6** pink monsters

HOW MANY MONSTERS HAVE **THREE EYES?**

There are
3
monsters with
three eyes!

HOW MANY MONSTERS HAVE **LEGS?**

There are

7

monsters
With legs!

HOW MANY MONSTERS HAVE **SPOTS?**

There are

8

monsters
with spots!

HOW MANY MONSTERS HAVE ONLY **ONE EYE?**

There are 5 monsters with only one eye!

ARE THERE MORE GREEN MONSTERS OR BLUE MONSTERS?

There are **9** green monsters and **9** blue monsters

So there are the **same amount** of **green** and **blue** monsters!

OUNT THE MONSTERS STICKING OUT THEIR TONGUES!

There are

6

monsters sticking out their tongues!

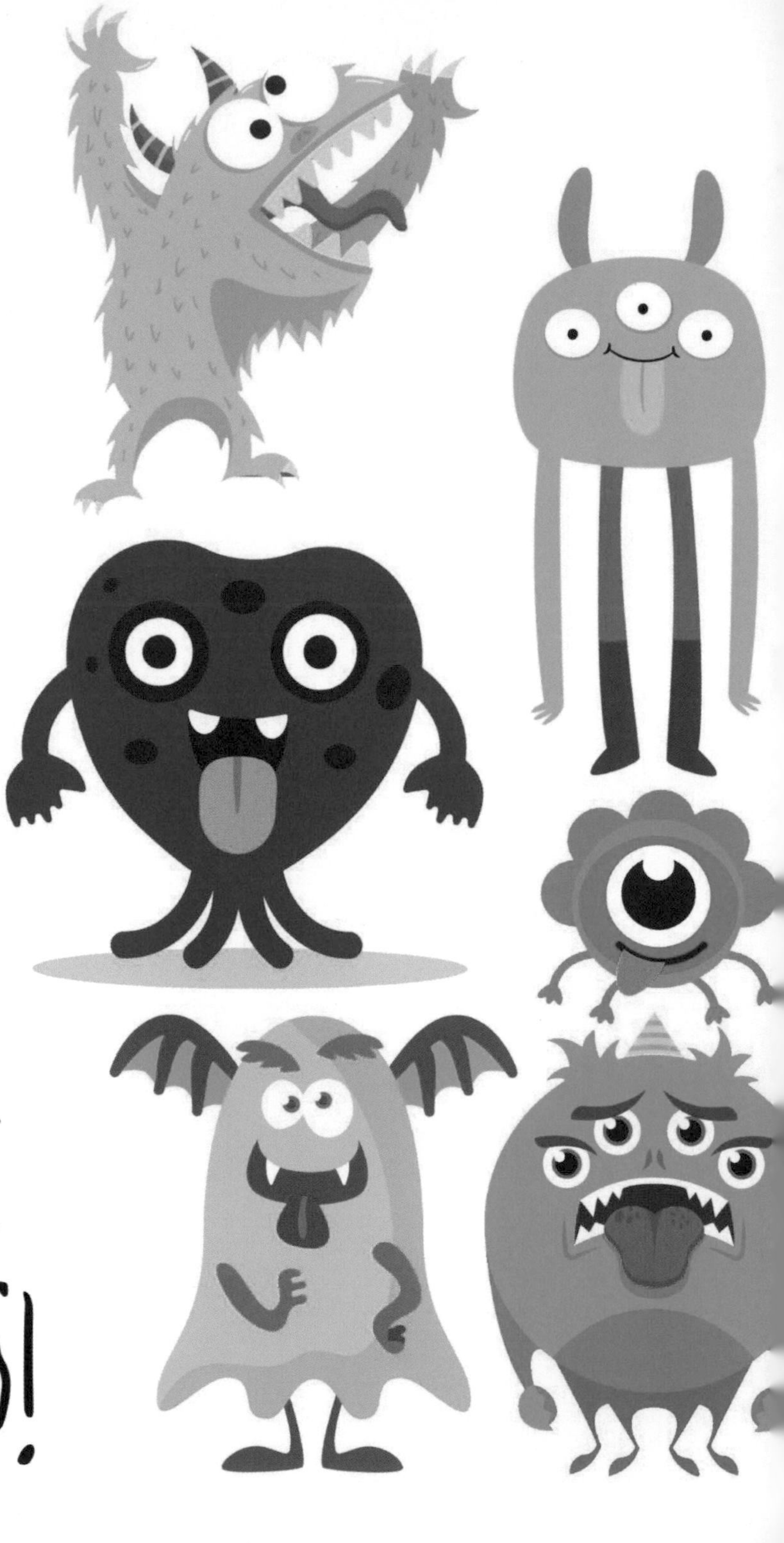

COUNT THE **HAPPY** MONSTERS!

There are 10 happy monsters!

HOW MANY MONSTERS HAVE **SHARP POINTY TEETH?**

There are **9** monsters with sharp pointy teeth!

ARE THERE MORE MONSTERS WAVING OR MONSTERS WITH WINGS?

There are **6** monsters with wings & there are **7** monsters waving.

So there are more

monsters waving!

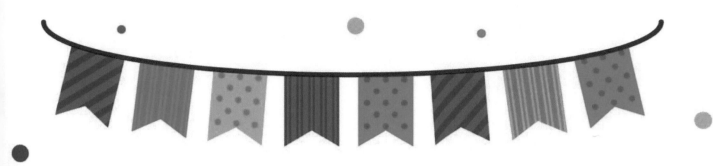

THE END!

BOOKS for little ONES

Find us on Amazon!

Discover all of the titles available in our store; including these below...

Why not try this awesome
monster activity book?

Full of mazes, wordsearches,
colouring pages and more!

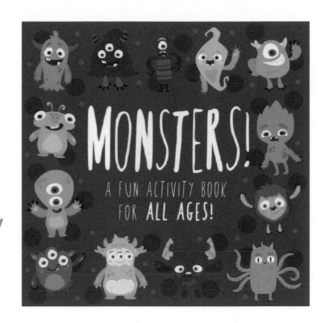

© 2018 Webber Books

Images and vectors by freepix, Macrovector, RosaPuchalt, brgfx, lexamer, stephanie2212, lesyaskripak, Ajipebriana, cornecoba, omegapics, Rayzong, layerace, ddraw, Vectortwins, Vector4free, anggar3ind, iconicbestiary, freshgraphix, natalka_dmitrova, Anindyanfitri, Alliesinteractive, bakar015, johndory, VVstudio, frimufilms, Emily_b, zirconicusso, gordoba

Printed in Great Britain
by Amazon